THREE MILE ISLAND

UNNATURAL DISASTERS

JULIE KNUTSON

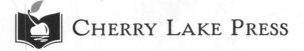

CHERRY LAKE PRESS

Published in the United States of America by Cherry Lake Publishing Group
Ann Arbor, Michigan
www.cherrylakepublishing.com

Reading Adviser: Marla Conn, MS, Ed., Literacy specialist, Read-Ability, Inc.
Photo Credits: © A. L. Spangler/Shutterstock.com, cover, 1; © Dobresum/Shutterstock.com, 5;
© Patriot-News library, 6; © Everett Collection/Shutterstock.com, 9, 11; © Stock Store/
Shutterstock.com, 12; © Syda Productions/Shutterstock.com, 15; © kuhn50/Shutterstock.com, 16;
© Doug McLean/Shutterstock.com, 19; © Joseph Sohm/Shutterstock.com, 20; © Bildagentur Zoonar
GmbH/Shutterstock.com, 23; © mark reinstein/Shutterstock.com, 24; © Fly_and_Dive/Shutterstock.com, 26

Cherry Lake Press is an imprint of Cherry Lake Publishing Group.

Library of Congress Cataloging-in-Publication Data
Names: Knutson, Julie, author.
Title: Three Mile Island / Julie Knutson.
Description: Ann Arbor, Michigan : Cherry Lake Publishing, 2021. | Series: Unnatural disasters : human
    error, design flaws, and bad decisions | Includes index. | Audience: Grades 4-6 | Summary: "Human
    modification of the environment always carries a risk of accident and folly. Explore the causes and
    consequences of the nuclear meltdown on Three Mile Island, Pennsylvania in 1979. Guided by compelling
    questions such as, "What led to this disaster?," "Who was impacted by it?," and "What changed in its
    aftermath?" the interdisciplinary content blends social studies and science. Ultimately, it pushes students
    to consider how humans can meet their need for resources in a safe, sustainable way. Books include
    table of contents, index, glossary, author biography, and timeline"– Provided by publisher.
Identifiers: LCCN 2020039989 (print) | LCCN 2020039990 (ebook) | ISBN 9781534180192 (hardcover) |
    ISBN 9781534181908 (paperback) | ISBN 9781534181205 (pdf) | ISBN 9781534182912 (ebook)
Subjects: LCSH: Nuclear power plants—Accidents—Pennsylvania—Juvenile literature. | Radioactive pollution—
    Pennsylvania—Juvenile literature. | Three Mile Island Nuclear Power Plant (Pa.)—Juvenile literature.
Classification: LCC TK9152 .K58 2021 (print) | LCC TK9152 (ebook) | DDC 363.17/990974818—dc23
LC record available at https://lccn.loc.gov/2020039989
LC ebook record available at https://lccn.loc.gov/2020039990

Cherry Lake Publishing Group would like to acknowledge the work of the Partnership for 21st Century
Learning, a Network of Battelle for Kids. Please visit http://www.battelleforkids.org/networks/p21
for more information.

Printed in the United States of America
Corporate Graphics

ABOUT THE AUTHOR

Julie Knutson is an Illinois-based author. In her spare moments, she enjoys investigating
new places and ideas alongside her husband, son, and border collie.

TABLE OF CONTENTS

"County Unprepared for Nuke Disaster"

On March 14, 1979, this chilling headline crept across the front page columns of the *York Daily Record*. Exactly 2 weeks later, residents of York and neighboring central Pennsylvania towns woke up to a nuclear nightmare. Just before 4 a.m. on March 28, 1979, many in the region surrounding the Three Mile Island (TMI) nuclear power plant reported hearing a loud boom. It wasn't until later that morning that they learned its cause.

At 8:25 a.m., local radio station WKBO broke the news that there had been an accident at TMI. By 9:06 a.m., word reached the Associated Press news agency. Soon, the world's attention was focused on events 10 miles (16 kilometers) from Pennsylvania's capital city, Harrisburg. What was happening at TMI? Would there be a full-blown nuclear catastrophe? What caused it? How would it impact the people living in the surrounding area?

Three Mile Island is in the Susquehanna River in Pennsylvania, about 14 miles (22.5 km) from the state capital of Harrisburg.

In the hours and days that followed, pregnant women and children were ordered to evacuate the area. Nervous kids waited for parents who scrambled to collect them from school. Emergency shelters were put in place. Residents received conflicting messages about the danger from leaked **radiation**. People speculated that if a **meltdown** happened, it would wipe out the entire eastern seaboard of the United States.

In an eerie coincidence, *The China Syndrome*, a movie about safety cover-ups at a nuclear plant, premiered 12 days before the partial meltdown at TMI.

The crisis ultimately passed without an explosion or immediate deaths. But cleanup lasted years, and its consequences didn't go away. It took a decade and more than $1 billion to **remediate**. It eroded the public's faith in the promise of nuclear technology as a safe, clean alternative to **fossil fuels**. It shook trust in government officials and corporations. And while some lessons were learned, not enough were—the world hadn't yet seen its most severe nuclear disasters.

[21ST CENTURY SKILLS LIBRARY]

Disaster Preparedness

What would people in the area around TMI do in the case of a nuclear accident? How aware was the public of evacuation plans? Journalists from the *York Daily Record* surveyed residents and reported their responses in the newspaper's March 14, 1979, issue. Selections from the Q&A follow:

Question: Have you heard or seen a copy of the evacuation plan for your area in case of a nuclear accident?

> **Answer:** "I didn't get a copy and didn't hear about it till I saw it over at my neighbor's. It's kind of scary."
>
> *– Mrs. Charlotte Neeper*
>
> **Answer:** "Don't you worry about an accident. You should be worried about nuclear attack. An accident can't happen."
>
> *– William O. Hunter*

Question: Do you remember what the plan is?

> **Answer:** "I received a plan with my taxes, though I can't say what it is. I guess praying would probably be my best bet."
>
> *– Martin Culver*

Before

It's Wednesday, January 23, 1957. Across America, excited children tune in to Walt Disney's *Wonderful World of Color*. Soon, the young viewers are whisked away on a televised, hour-long journey from the ancient past to the future. It centers on getting better acquainted with "our friend, the atom."

The show aired just over 10 years after the United States dropped the atomic bomb on Hiroshima and Nagasaki, Japan, during World War II. Image makers like Walt Disney were looking to reinvent perceptions of the atom's power. Disney's presentation— and countless others—set out to convince the public that atomic energy wasn't just capable of destruction. It could also be harnessed for good, to create a clean and energy-efficient future.

The destruction of the Japanese city Nagasaki showed the world the terrible power of the atom.

Cities, airplanes, trains, medicine, and agriculture could all be fueled by the process of **nuclear fission**. It could open the door to a better tomorrow.

The United States had managed to keep its military nuclear technology secret for a time. But soon, other world powers used atomic science to begin building not just weapons, but also power stations. In these settings, fission was controlled to produce electricity.

Discovering Fission

Nuclear fission was discovered by a team of scientists in 1938. Lise Meitner, Otto Hahn, and Fritz Strassmann bombarded a uranium atom with neutrons. They managed to successfully split the atom's **nucleus**. Opportunities for harnessing the split atom's energy were enormous. Germany's Nazi regime recognized the potential to turn this technology into a weapon, and government scientists were commissioned to build an atomic bomb.

In a 1939 letter, Albert Einstein reported this news to President Roosevelt. The United States quickly responded, creating the Manhattan Project to build a nuclear weapon of its own. Spread across multiple states and laboratory sites, the U.S. team conducted the first nuclear test in New Mexico on July 16, 1945. Less than one month later, the technology was used to bomb the Japanese cities of Hiroshima and Nagasaki. The true **casualty** toll of the bombings will never be known, but low estimates place the number of dead and wounded around 225,000.

The world's first nuclear reactor was built in Chicago in 1942 as part of the Manhattan Project. The reactor was underneath the University of Chicago's football stadium.

Enriched uranium fuel rods were suspended in a pool of water and bombarded with neutrons to produce a **chain reaction**. This had the effect of heating the surrounding water, which produced steam. That steam propelled turbines, which produced electricity that powered an entire **grid**.

The world's first nuclear power plant debuted in the Soviet Union in 1954. A power station in England followed in 1956. The United States got into the business in 1958, when the Shippingport Atomic Power Station opened in western Pennsylvania. But even as nuclear construction projects took root across the country,

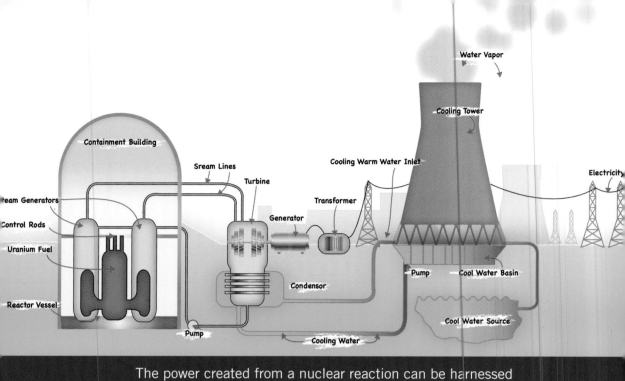

The power created from a nuclear reaction can be harnessed to generate a large amount of electrical energy.

some people weren't convinced. Early protests of power stations near Detroit and San Francisco showed that not everyone was eager to get friendly with "our friend the atom."

As the **Cold War** grew more intense in the 1950s and 1960s, the anti-nuclear movement grew. People feared the possibility of a nuclear missile attack. At school, American children routinely practiced "duck-and-cover" drills. These drills involved rehearsing what to do in case of a nuclear explosion. With the birth of the environmental and peace movements in the late 1960s and early 1970s, anti-nuclear attitudes gained even more support. And with the relatively cheap cost of fossil fuels, there wasn't a good reason to take on the risks of using nuclear energy.

A turning point in the early 1970s allowed the promise of an atomic age to return. In 1973, the Organization of the Petroleum Exporting Countries placed limits on how much oil could be sold to the United States. With its fuel-inefficient vehicles, the country wasn't prepared for this move. Gas prices surged. Massive shortages were reported. Motorists waited in long lines to fuel their cars, only to find that the filling station had run out of gas. An energy-independent future fueled by **domestic** nuclear power suddenly looked more appealing.

The years between 1970 and 1985 saw a nuclear power building boom. More than half of the reactors in the world were built during this period. A 1975 Harris poll showed that 63 percent of Americans supported building more nuclear plants to meet energy needs. Construction on TMI's cooling towers began just before this time, in 1968.

The Accident

"There was a run on the banks. Teenagers were going around town announcing that everyone had to evacuate. It was a mess. I recall standing on a street corner. People were hollering out of their car windows, 'Mayor, watch the town!' I knew I couldn't go. I kept thinking, I was born and raised here. If we had a heavy release of radiation, I'd have to leave this area and start a new life somewhere else. A lot of people thought about this. 'What's going to happen to us? Where are we going to go?'"

— former Middletown, Pennsylvania, Mayor Robert Reid (Smithsonian Magazine, April 2019)

Travel back in time to late March 1979. It's a Friday afternoon. Suddenly, your principal barges into your classroom. He rushes to the windows and pulls all the curtains shut. The explanation given

Closing blinds at the school probably wouldn't have done much to keep radiation out. Radioactive substances can linger in the air and settle in soil and water, impacting entire ecosystems.

to you and your 11-year-old classmates? There's been a nuclear accident, and this will keep the radiation out. There are no cell phones, so a quick text to check in with your parents isn't an option. There's no internet or email. The news that you and your family gets comes through the radio, newspaper, or television. Getting in touch with a family member would require a landline telephone. You're stuck waiting. You wonder what's going on outside that window. You're seized with worry for yourself, your family, neighbors, and pets.

Cooling towers at Three Mile Island.

The crisis at TMI's Unit 2 reactor began around 4 a.m. on Wednesday, March 28. A chain reaction had occurred at the plant, but not the kind that was supposed to happen. A water pump linked to the plant's cooling system experienced a minor glitch. In response, the reactor shut down. Pressure in the pipes connected to the reactor increased. Control room equipment showed that a key release valve that controlled the pressure in these pipes was sealed shut. In reality, the valve was stuck open, allowing water and steam to pour out. This valve stayed open for 2 hours as staff scrambled to figure out what was happening.

All the while, the facility's core, where the uranium rods were housed, were overheating. The radioactive materials encased within were melting. As people would later learn, trace amounts of radiation escaped into the atmosphere.

TMI's Unit 2 reactor had only been up and running a few months before the accident. Construction lasted from 1969 to 1978. It began operating alongside Unit 1, which opened in 1974, on December 30, 1978. Together, TMI's units could power electricity to 500,000 to 1 million area homes.

At local radio station WKBO, news anchor Mike Pintek received word from a traffic reporter that emergency vehicles were heading toward TMI. Pintek called TMI and was patched through to the control room. On the other end of the line, he heard alarms and frantic voices. As Pintek later told a *National Geographic* documentary crew, the TMI employee who answered said, "I can't talk now, we've got a problem." At 8:25 a.m., he broke the news to local listeners that officials at Met-Ed (the company that operated TMI) "had to shut down their Three Mile Island nuclear power station unit number two . . . after an accident occurred within the plant's turbine system. Officials have been saying that there is no danger to the general public and the situation is under control."

Met-Ed downplayed the situation. At the same time, local and state government officials scrambled to advise citizens about evacuations. Scientists from the Nuclear Regulatory Commission (NRC) were called in to assess the situation. At 9:15 a.m., the White House was briefed. For people in the region, there were infinite questions and very few clear answers. As Met-Ed spokespeople assured the public that there was no immediate risk from the accident, some residents went about life as usual. On Thursday, high school students in towns near the site could be spotted carrying **Geiger counters** to measure the radioactivity in rainwater puddles.

A Geiger counter measures radiation in micro-Sieverts (uSv).
One uSv equals one-millionth of a Sievert.

On Friday, March 30, the situation changed yet again. A potentially explosive hydrogen bubble was discovered in the containment building. The bubble could interfere with efforts to cool the core that suffered loss of liquid 2 days earlier. Making matters worse, it could also explode if too much oxygen entered the chamber.

Jimmy Carter was president of the United States from 1977 to 1981. His visit to TMI after the crisis convinced citizens the danger there was over.

That afternoon, Pennsylvania Governor Richard Thornburgh ordered an evacuation for all pregnant women and preschool-age children living within a 5-mile (8 km) radius of TMI. In reality, the mayor of nearby Middletown estimated that three-quarters of residents fled the area. As they crammed belongings into suitcases, many wondered if they'd ever return home again.

It was an anxious, fretful weekend. Pennsylvanians waited and watched to see if the bubble would shrink. Good news finally came as temperatures in the reactor core dropped. There was no oxygen in the chamber that could cause an explosion. The threat, it seemed, had passed.

The following day, Sunday, April 1, President Jimmy Carter—a former naval officer who had experience working with nuclear technology—visited the plant. His tour of the grounds eased fears about the situation. Many felt that if the TMI area was safe enough for the U.S. president and his advisers, the risk had likely passed. At a press conference at Middletown's borough hall, Carter assured the media and local leaders that he'd been told the area was "quite safe for all concerned."

In July 1979, an accident at Church Rock, a uranium mine in New Mexico, released even more radioactive material than TMI. A dam wall at a processing mill burst, releasing 94 million gallons of liquid radioactive waste and 1,100 tons of solid waste into Rio Puerco, a crucial source of water for residents. The accident's effects on members of the Navajo Nation living in the area went largely uncovered by the media and ignored by the government. Today, cleanup work is still ongoing, and activists are still fighting for environmental justice and the universal right to a healthy, safe environment.

After

The partial meltdown at TMI's Unit 2 was among the worst nuclear accidents in U.S. history. Cleanup took 14 years and cost more than $1 billion. Damage couldn't fully be measured for several years. Close inspection of the radioactive core was too risky for humans, so a team of engineers from Carnegie Mellon University built camera-equipped robots to do the work. These robots scoped the site and collected samples. Imaging showed that the core was more damaged than expected. While experts first estimated that 1 percent of rods melted, in reality, it was closer to 50 percent. Radioactive fuel and water were removed from the site and are now stored at the U.S. Department of Energy's Idaho National Laboratory. Radioactive material that could not safely be removed from the damaged reactor was sealed in concrete on the site.

Today, nuclear power accounts for 10.4 percent of the world's energy. It makes up more than 70 percent of energy in France. Above is a nuclear plant in Cattenom, France.

While most residents who evacuated returned within a week or two, some people never came back. For those living in the shadows of TMI, getting back to "normal" was a long process.

Many who survived the ordeal became anti-nuclear activists. And even though health officials offered assurances that the amount of radiation released was too small to cause harm, many wondered if they would suffer lasting health impacts. More than a half dozen studies showed no increase of cancer or other diseases. But research from Penn State University's Hershey campus in 2017 suggested higher rates of thyroid cancer in those exposed.

"No Nukes" protests erupted all over the country after the TMI crisis. There was even a "No Nukes" concert at Madison Square Garden featuring Bruce Springsteen & the E Street Band and Tom Petty & the Heartbreakers.

The events at TMI led to anti-nuclear attitudes and protests. As a result, the growing nuclear industry came to a screeching halt. Between 1979 and 1988, construction was canceled on 68 planned nuclear facilities in the United States alone. The 1986 disaster at the Chernobyl nuclear power station in Ukraine—a full meltdown that spread radioactive particles across Europe—cemented public fear and distrust. It took decades for those feelings to fade. But by the 2000s, people were again looking to nuclear power as a clean, efficient source of energy. In 2010, President Obama announced

[21ST CENTURY SKILLS LIBRARY]

that, for the first time in 30 years, the country would invest $8.3 billion to build new reactors. Then, a year later, another major nuclear catastrophe happened in Japan.

The Chernobyl plant was built in Soviet-controlled Ukraine between 1977 and 1983. The radioactive fallout released by the Chernobyl disaster is estimated at 300 to 400 times that generated by the atomic bomb at Hiroshima.

On March 11, 2011, a magnitude 9.0 earthquake struck Japan. It was the most powerful earthquake ever recorded in the island nation's history. That violent quake was followed by an equally violent **tsunami**. Damage caused by these twin natural disasters led to an emergency at the Fukushima Daiichi Nuclear Power Plant. As at TMI, Fukushima's cooling system was damaged. The tsunami's waves also flooded the buildings with seawater. The plant experienced three nuclear meltdowns and three hydrogen explosions. It was the second-worst nuclear accident in history, after Chernobyl.

The earthquake and tsunami that caused the Fukushima disaster also caused widespread damage across the region.

Just over 40 years after the accident at TMI, the plant's remaining Unit 1 reactor closed. Exelon Corp., the facility's operator since 1998, cited financial reasons. Uranium rods from the active part of the plant were retired to spent fuel pools for cooling. Once cooled, they'll join radioactive material from Unit 2's core in Idaho. The **decommissioning** process will take up to 6 decades and cost another $1 billion.

After TMI, Chernobyl, and Fukushima, is the dream of nuclear energy dead? Today, some experts argue that its potential benefits outweigh its risks. To these observers, the relatively small risk of an accident has to be balanced against the certainty of climate change, population growth, and increasing energy demands. Others think that renewables like solar and wind power might hold the answer. **Nuclear fusion** is another proposed possibility.

What kind of future do *you* want to see? What future do you want to help create?

Research & Act

The severity of nuclear incidents is measured on a scale ranging from 1 to 7. TMI is regarded as a 5, an "accident with wider consequences." Chernobyl and Fukushima are considered to be level 7, major accidents. Conduct more research to learn about the meltdowns at Chernobyl and Fukushima. Investigate the *who*, *what*, *when*, *where*, *why*, and *how* of both events. Were they preventable? What changes happened after they occurred? Could an event like this happen again?

Next, write an editorial arguing "for" or "against" nuclear power. Have we learned enough from the past to safely use this technology? Share and discuss your findings with family members and teachers. Ask for their viewpoints on nuclear power. Do they have any memories of these three accidents? If so, how do they shape their perspectives?

Timeline

December 1938: German scientists discover the process of nuclear fission.

August 1945: The United States drops atomic bombs over the Japanese cities of Hiroshima and Nagasaki.

1954: The world's first nuclear power plant opens in Russia.

May 1968: Construction begins on Unit 1 at TMI.

December 1978: Unit 2 at TMI begins operating.

March 28, 1979: Around 4 a.m., an accident in Unit 2 sparks a partial meltdown.

March 30, 1979: Pregnant women and preschool-age children are advised to evacuate the area.

April 26, 1986: The worst nuclear disaster in history occurs in Chernobyl, Ukraine.

March 11, 2011: An earthquake and tsunami lead to the Fukushima Daiichi nuclear disaster in Japan.

September 2019: TMI closes completely.

Further Research

Fasick, Erik V. *Three Mile Island*. Charleston, SC: Arcadia Publishing, 2019.

LaMar, Scott. *Meltdown at Three Mile Island: 40 Years Later*. PBS, March 26, 2019, www.pbs.org/video/meltdown-at-three-mile-island-40-years-later-yj2jx2/.

Lusted, Marcia Amidon. *The Three Mile Island Nuclear Disaster*. Minneapolis, MN: ABDO Publishing. Company, 2012.

Roane, Kit R. *Nuclear Power's Promise and Peril*. *The New York Times*, April 28, 2014, www.nytimes.com/video/us/100000002847044/nuclear-power-promise-and-peril.html.

"Three Mile Island Accident" on *Letter from America by Alistair Cooke*, BBC Radio 4 podcast, April 6, 1976.

Glossary

casualty (KAZH-oo-uhl-tee) a person killed or injured

chain reaction (CHAYN ree-AK-shuhn) a series of events that are triggered by one initial event

Cold War (KOHLD WOR) the period of tension between the United States and former Soviet Union that lasted from about 1945 until 1990

decommissioning (dee-kuh-MISH-uhn-ing) taking something fully out of use

domestic (duh-MES-tik) produced or made within a country

enriched (en-RICHD) enhanced or improved with something else

fossil fuels (FAH-suhl FYOO-uhlz) natural fuels such as coal or gas, formed out of the remains of living organisms

Geiger counters (GYE-gur KOUNT-urz) tools used to detect radioactivity

grid (GRID) a network that delivers electricity from power plants to consumers (houses, schools, businesses)

meltdown (MELT-doun) an accident in a nuclear reactor that happens when the fuel overheats and melts the surrounding core and equipment

nuclear fission (NOO-klee-ur FISH-uhn) the process of splitting an atom to create energy

nuclear fusion (NOO-klee-ur FYOO-zhuhn) the process of fusing two atoms together to create energy

nucleus (NOO-klee-uhs) the dense core of the atom that contains protons and neutrons

radiation (ray-dee-AY-shuhn) the process of giving off energy in rays or particles

remediate (rih-MEE-dee-ate) to fix or correct

tsunami (tsu-NAH-mee) a giant sea wave caused by an earthquake or other disturbance

uranium (yu-RAY-nee-uhm) dense radioactive metal that is used as fuel in nuclear reactors

INDEX